GW00503693

Shipping Container Homes

Great Shipping Container House Ideas

Table of Contents

The Newest Trend in Housing Design

When businessman and ex-driver Malcolm McLean patented the first shipping containers in the 1950's, he was only looking to improve how freight was carried on cargo ships.

Back in those days, it took a week for an average ship to be fully loaded or unloaded since the cargo was packaged in individual pieces. Remembering how inefficient this was and not wanting to apply the same system in his new haulage business, McLean came up with the idea to use containers to carry cargo in bulk. These containers could be handled quickly by crane and would reduce the loading and unloading time significantly. Thus, the shipping container was born.

This innovation revolutionized the shipping industry when it first appeared, more than 50 years ago. Now, shipping containers (also known as ISO containers) are the norm for freight transport around the world.

But little did McLean know that his invention would be used for more purposes than he intended. Because they are inexpensive, easily obtainable, and very sturdy, shipping containers are now being used in architecture around the world.

They have now been utilized to construct almost everything: from emergency shelters and shopping malls to military training facilities and bank vaults. People all over the world have seen the potential of shipping containers in construction.

In particular, there has been an upsurge in the construction of shipping container homes. Architects and amateur home designers have taken up the challenge of converting these steel boxes into homes that are innovative, practical, and even luxurious.

As a material for construction, shipping containers have many advantages that contribute to its recent popularity with homebuilders and designers.

They are sturdy and durable

Because they are built to handle heavy loads, shipping containers have a strength and durability that is virtually unmatched in the filed of ready-made materials. They are also meant to be stacked, which means they can handle a fair amount of weight. One container is a structurally sound base for more containers piled on top of it. This makes for interesting and endless design possibilities for multi-level homes.

In addition, shipping containers were also built to handle the battering of the elements. This makes for a sturdy and secure home that can potentially withstand even the harshest of environmental conditions with the right design and construction.

They are modular

This means that they can be combined or connected in numerous ways.

As a rule, all shipping containers are identical in width and follow standard height and length measurements. This uniformity of shape and size makes it easy to interlock multiple containers into a stable structure, a valuable attribute in the shipping industry and an added advantage in house construction.

Because of this stability and modularity, construction is relatively easier and making additions to an existing structure can be as easy as adding and stacking more containers.

They require less labor

Unlike the conventional construction of homes using wood, cement, or brick, building a house out of shipping containers requires specialized labor. Since these containers are made of steel, majority of the labor will be divided between welding and steel cutting.

While these jobs cost more than conventional house-building tasks, in the end, there is less work to be done. The overall expense on labor will usually be lower than the average labor expense for regular homes.

They are accessible and easily transported

Because their original use is for transport, shipping containers already follow standard shipping requirements. This means that they can be transported easily through any means, whether by ship, truck, or rail.

However, transport really isn't a pressing concern. In most cases, it will not be necessary. Shipping containers are available literally everywhere around the world. Each city with an operational port or major transport dock will most likely have shipping containers available for sale.

They are less expensive

Constructing a house from shipping containers is undoubtedly less expensive than buying or building a conventional home. As previously mentioned, the labor costs are significantly less. Also, it is possible to obtain used shipping containers for as low as $1,200 in the United States. A brand new one will typically cost less than $6,000. In comparison, the materials for regular homes (such as mortar or brick) are significantly more expensive.

These advantages are notable and well worth consideration. However, as in any type of build, there are a few things that are worth additional attention when constructing a shipping container home versus an average home.

Insulation and Sealing

A shipping container home will have to be insulated better than most wood, brick, or block structures, especially in environments with high temperatures. The containers are made of steel and conduct heat very efficiently, so to prevent extreme heat inside the home, proper insulation is necessary.

In temperate climates, high humidity can also be a problem. Rust may form when the moist air in the interior condenses against the steel walls of the shipping container. But this will not be a problem with adequate sealing and insulation.

Construction Equipment and Tools

Because this is not the typical housing build, it requires special equipment and tools that are uncommon in most construction sites for regular homes. In particular, equipment for welding and steel-cutting will be needed.

A forklift or crane will also be required to move the shipping containers, since the size and weight of these materials make it impossible to move them by hand, unlike typical materials like lumber or brick.

Building Permits

Although they have been gaining popularity, shipping container homes are still relatively rare and their construction may be unprecedented in a few regions. Add that to the use of steel—which is common for industrial construction but not for residential—and it may be harder than usual to obtain a building permit.

Flooring Treatments and Possible Contaminants

Some countries have laws that require wood floors of shipping containers to be treated with insecticides to avoid infestations. For example, in Australia, shipping container floors are treated with insecticides that contain 38-45% chromium, 30-37% arsenic, and 23-25% copper.

These chemicals can be detrimental to humans as well. To avoid health risks, floors should be removed and replaced before habitation, or better yet, shipping containers with steel flooring can be utilized instead.

Also, shipping containers are used as transport for a wide variety of materials and contamination or spillage is inevitable. It is very important to clean them thoroughly before they are utilized in construction, especially in the case of pre-owned and used containers. Additionally, since these containers were not manufactured with human habitation in mind, the paints and sealants used may not be up to human safety standards.

To avoid health hazards, it is ideal to perform abrasive blasting on all the surfaces of the container until only bare metal is left. After this, the uncontaminated surface can be repainted with nontoxic paint.

Structural Damage and Weaknesses

When opting for used containers, do not forget to inspect for any damages to the container. Typically, they are only condemned if there are faults to be found, so be sure to know what these faults are. Damages like twisted frames or cracked welds can compromise the structural integrity of the container and will need to be remedied.

It is also important to note that while the ends of a container are durable to the extreme because of the reinforcements made to the corners, the roof, while sturdy, is not as heavy-duty. Without reinforcement, any additional weight placed on top of it should preferably be less than 300 pounds per square foot.

Remember that just like any construction project, building a shipping container home is best accomplished with the correct information and preparation.

Things to Consider Before Construction

Planning is the real key to a build that is efficient, economical, and achievable. Even before coming up with a design plan, there are many factors that need to be considered. Proper preparation ensures that the build goes smoothly when it is actually under way.

In the Pre-Design stage, the goal is to come up with the concept for the design. The input of those involved in the actual construction—including designers, contractors, and equipment or material suppliers—is taken into account, along with the expectations of the future homeowners and the money they are willing to spend.

All in all, this will result in a complete profile of the project: the scope, the budget, and the risks and difficulties to be potentially experienced during the build.

That said, figuring out were to begin can be daunting, especially for a first construction project. Following a checklist (like the one shown here) can be a great way to get started.

Go see an actual shipping container

Obviously, shipping containers are needed to build a shipping container home. That is why the first step is to find an actual container and give it a thorough examination. Get a concrete idea of what the space really looks like. This will help in figuring out the overall design later and in keeping expectations in the realm of the feasible.

This is also a chance to compare the quality and price of containers from different sources, should there be more than one in an area. When surveying used containers, keep an eye out for ones that have minimal damage. These may cost a little more, but it is better than going cheap and then overspending on repairs.

Review building regulations and construction codes that apply to the prospective building site

A lot will depend on the location of the build. Contact the local building or planning department and inquire about mandatory permits and inspections, as well as any building restrictions. Mention that the home to be constructed has modular steel components and ask if this will lead to any pre-construction issues.

As a rule, most governing bodies grant landowners the right to build almost any type of residence on privately owned property. However, in some cases a Certificate of Occupancy may be required. To obtain it, it is necessary to follow building and zoning regulations.

Height limitations, maximum square footage, even the number of bathrooms allowed, are all examples of the kind of information that is vital in coming up with a final design.

Determine the budget

It's easy to just name a price and call it the budget, but really, that's not how things should be done.

Coming up with a budget requires a look at *every* aspect of the build. Get an idea of the construction, labor, and professional fees. Take note of everything that needs to be done, what materials will be required and exactly how many people will be needed. Minimize the risk of incurring unexpected expenses by being as thorough as possible.

Consulting architects and contractors is a great way to get a more concrete idea of how much a project will cost. It is also advisable to get in contact with companies who sell containers and do modifications.

It is best to keep the budget a little below the amount of money that is actually available. This margin will cover any unanticipated expenses that are to be expected during any construction project.

Do a physical survey of the building site

As previously mentioned, the choice of building site is crucial. One big factor to consider is the soil bearing capacity—referring to the capacity of the soil to support the structural load applied to the ground.

Other features of the site, such as the landscape and greenery, can be taken advantage of to provide not only an aesthetic appeal, but a practical one as well. For example, clumps of trees can naturally provide shade and decrease winter chill when taken into account in design.

The location of a house will also determine the ease of access and the degree of privacy. Try to see how far the site is from the road or highway. Will it be necessary to add an extended driveway? Concerns like this can increase the cost of the build and should be taken into account during budgeting.

Decide on the exact project requirements

Get started on a "wish list". In particular, focus on the number of rooms that are needed. Decide on how many bedrooms and bathrooms there will be, and on whether rooms will be constructed for utilities like the kitchen and dinning area. Detail any additional features desired, such as a home office space, a game room or the like. Make an estimate of the rough square footage required for each, and for the whole project.

However, prepare to negotiate. Most likely, adjustments will need to be made in coming up with the final design or during the course of the build. Try your best to be flexible and to be open to new ideas and suggestions from professionals.

Create a layout and floor plan.

Once the "wish list" is ready, start sketching a layout and floor plan for the home. Make sure to draw the dimensions to scale. This will give a better idea of what the finished product will actually look like after completion.

Remember to incorporate *all* the functional elements that should be in the home, outlining the correct number of rooms and their purpose. Incorporate as many ideas as possible, but don't overcrowd the space. The key to a comfortable living area is a balanced utilization of space. Even a room with a small area can feel relatively expansive with a successful interior layout.

Finalize the design

A general idea is all well and good, but once that's done, it's time to get into the specifics. There are a few ways to go about designing a shipping container home.

One is to hire an architect to come up with the design based on the outlined specifications. This has the advantage of producing a completely unique and original home that will cater to specific needs or preferences.

However, there is a downside. Since shipping container homes are still relatively rare, it may be a challenge to find someone who is willing and able to design the home. There are many design considerations unique to shipping container homes that the average architect—no matter how skilled—may be unfamiliar with.

An alternative is to locate a design entity that offers turnkey home designs. "Turnkey" means the design is ready to use once purchased. The source company will offer several "stock" designs to choose from. These ready-made "kit" designs can then be adapted to the building site.

Although this doesn't allow for extensive customization, it has the advantage of taking less time and costing less overall. Should there be non-negotiable aspects of the home, which should *absolutely* be included in the design, look for a company who is willing to customize, although this will probably increase the cost.

Additionally, having the final design is essential in coming up with the final budget. These plans and drawings, among other documents, are also needed in applying for building permits and getting authorization for construction.

Constructing a Shipping Container Home

The design is ready, permits have been obtained and submitted, and materials and equipment have been ordered. Once these preparations are complete, it is time for the build to get under way. This is a crucial stage, where the project leaves the confines of pen and paper and the actual shipping container home is materialized.

Building a house is by all means an easy task. Things won't always go according to plan and at some point the build *will* encounter problems, but that is true for all construction projects. Don't panic and don't stress.

Even if a third party, such as a general contractor, is doing the work, get involved. Ask how things are going and check out the site from time to time.

Following along these guidelines will help keep things on track.

Prepare the building site

Preliminary work on the building site includes the excavation and grading for the foundation and utilities like electrical, water, and gas lines. Depending on the design, additional preparation might be necessary. Storm water management systems and septic systems are a few common additions.

Lay down the foundations

The type of foundation is also dependent upon the design. In general, concrete is used as foundation for shipping container homes. This can be poured or placed as premade blocks. Precast panels are also available from factories, many already insulated, water proofed, and ready to use.

The process of laying the foundations is similar to that of conventional construction. Lines for utilities are laid at the base, foundation walls are filled, soil is compacted on top, a layer of gravel is added, rebar is set in place, and a slab of concrete is poured out.

Ready the shipping containers

Shipping containers need to be modified before they can be used for home construction. As mentioned in previous chapters, the expense of steel construction is higher than that of wood or others. To mitigate the cost, it is advisable to have as many modifications done off-site as possible. Re-sellers of shipping containers usually have facilities that can make modifications.

Although shipping containers are much stronger than materials for most homes, making alterations to the structure can compromise its integrity. Cutting holes and removing parts can cause it to weaken.

To avoid safety hazards, be sure to consult an architect or structural engineer on the level of modification. Some reinforcement may be necessary to stabilize the structure.

Set the containers on the foundation and against each other

Once the foundation and the containers are ready, it is time to put them together.

Containers will need to be crane-lifted on the foundation one by one. They are then hooked in place and the bottom corners are welded to the foundation to keep the structure secure. Metal plates are embedded into the foundation to provide areas of attachment for the containers.

Depending on how they will be arranged or stacked, these containers will also be welded to each other. The corners are the strongest part of the container, so it is best to weld these areas together as much as possible for maximum stability.

Install doors, windows, and other panels to cover openings

The first thing to do is to measure and cut the openings where doors and windows will be placed. As much as possible, these should be done off-site, however they can be done on-site if necessary. These openings should be framed with hollow rectangle steel sections to prevent from weakening the structure. A steel L section can also be used.

This is not limited to doors and windows. Other additional openings, such as skylights, should be treated in the same fashion as well.

Install plumbing and electrical systems, heating and cooling systems, insulation, and fixtures

When the overall structure is set up, it is time to get to work on the interior of the home. Installing electrical wiring, plumbing, and heating and cooling systems are pretty much the same in a shipping container home as it is in a conventional one.

For insulation, a high-performance, four-part ceramic isolative coating called supertherm is recommended. It is sprayed on both the inside and outside walls of the container to protect it from extreme fluctuations in temperature.

Drywall is applied to the inner walls and as interior partitions. Additional vertical supports may also be added. Install any additional fixtures.

Once this is done, the house is basically finished!

Do a final inspection

After everything is finalized, inspect the result with the contractor and a building official. Check *everything*, from the foundation to the architecture, to the plumbing and electrical systems and even the grade and landscaping around the home. This is an important step, because it is much easier to remedy any errors sooner rather than later.

The approval of a building official will be necessary in the application for a Certificate of Occupancy.

By the end of this process, a house will have been produced from steel boxes that were previously only used to carry and transport various things. Now, all it needs are occupants to turn it from a house into a home.

Design Ideas to Choose From

Design is an integral part of any construction project, especially in a home. The right design can showcase the personality of the occupants at a glance while still being functional and practical.

Generally, there are two ways to design a structure: to impose it upon a landscape, or to let it embrace the landscape. Depending on the future homeowner's preference, each method will produce a stunning home within a comparable budget.

Embracing the site comes with restrictions on the design. That being said, taking the environment into account and using it to ones' advantage has its perks. A home that makes use of natural lighting and natural buffers against the elements (like forests) will need significantly less heating and cooling, which means less expense.

Imposing a design has the advantage of having more freedom with the actual look of the structure. The home can have the exact detailing that future homeowners want, and can better accommodate any specific needs or demands. However, it requires a more active heating and cooling system.

In the end, preference will dictate the design. With shipping container homes, the possibilities are limitless. This is part of their appeal and the reason why more and more architects and homebuilders are coming up with designs for shipping container homes around the world. This new trend is an avenue to showcase unparalleled creativity and innovation.

With so many options, deciding on which direction to go can be a bit overwhelming. To help narrow down the field, here's a list of a few design options to choose from. They don't even need to be mutually exclusive. Don't be afraid to mix and match ideas!

The Industrial Look

For shipping container homes, this type of design is a shoo-in. Their structure naturally lends them to this kind of style. Their geometrically defined rectangular shape is great when unmodified and shows the clean, simplistic lines characteristic of this style.

The interior as well, is easily done to this style. For example, the corrugated steel walls are usually covered with drywall, but cleaning them up and repainting them (or keeping them bare) is actually a great design statement. This is best done for sections of the wall, functioning as accents, rather than for all of the walls.

Stacking It Up: Multi-Levels

One of the greatest advantages of using shipping containers as a building material is that they are modular and naturally very stable when arranged or stacked against each other. This opens up many possibilities in terms of design.

The result is the creation of multi-level shipping container homes that are not only expansive and spacious with great square-footage, but also eye-catching and architecturally interesting as well. There are so many ways to arrange these containers into exciting shapes and structures; the possibilities are limited only by the imagination.

However, don't forget to make sure that the design is structurally sound by having it examined by professional architects and engineers.

Going Big

Because they are easy to arrange and stack, as previously mentioned, it is actually a simple matter to create a relatively large structure from multiple containers.

In 2010, a French architect named Patrick Partouche designed a home with 2,240 square feet from several shipping containers. This is only one example among many that exist today. Outside of residential projects, shipping containers have been used to build shopping malls and Starbucks shops!

For an expansive home, with spacious living areas, going big is the best choice. And as a bonus, building a big home from shipping containers costs much less than conventional construction of the same scale.

Going Small

If a big home is too much of a commitment (or a little over-budget), then it might be a great option to downsize and go smaller. This is especially true if only one or two individuals will occupy the house. A functional home can be made with two or even just one shipping container. It will be enough for basic necessities and utilities. Some resorts even offer converted shipping containers as their private suites and cabins.

Additionally, starting with a small project is a great way to get familiar with the building process. Before starting on a shipping container *home*, it might be good to get a feel of the build by trying for a shipping container art studio or guest house first.

Eco-friendly And Natural

There are probably few applications of the "Reduce, Reuse, Recycle" motto that are more radical than converting a used shipping container into a house. It is the ultimate display of commitment to environmental conservation. Not only does this recycle the used containers, it also gives them a vital purpose that will keep them useful for many, many years to come.

A good number of shipping container homeowners *are* environmentally conscious, and this has affected their decision to go ahead and build their homes in this way. Some have taken the next step and made their homes even more eco-friendly by relying on solar power, having rainwater collection systems, using recycled materials as furnishings, and more.

The "look" of the house can reflect the commitment to nature and the environment as well. Designs that integrated reclaimed wood, sustainable bamboo, and recycled metal are not at all uncommon for this type of construction.

Making It Fun with Color

Vibrant, loud colors can add a touch of whimsy to *any* structure, but especially to shipping container homes.

Since the shape of the structure itself is already unique and quirky, adding a pop of bright color can bring that extra element of fun to a shipping container home. It's a great attraction for kids and those who enjoy a youthful and energetic vibe.

Some homes have little to no structural modification on the shipping containers, but a splash of color is enough to turn an old steel box into an inviting, fun and unique retreat that showcases the personality of the occupants.

Not a Container House at All

For homeowners who are fans of the traditional style, it is perfectly possible to build a shipping container home that looks like the average, conventional residence.

With the right design and modifications, a shipping container home will look indistinguishable among the houses of an urban suburb. If that's a little *too* plain and ordinary, these materials easily lend themselves to a touch of creativity and modernity that will elevate the home from being just the average "normal" house.

Prefabricated and Mobile

There are people who are not at all picky with design and would prefer a quick build with minimal problems and uncertainties. For these individuals, a prefabricated shipping container home may be the best option.

Many companies these days sell prefabricated homes that are easy to build and will be up and running as functioning houses within days or even hours. While, not custom, these designs still look very appealing and are homes to be proud of.

In addition, many of these prefabricated options are also mobile, so for people who travel a lot and are always on the go, this may be the perfect alternative to a conventional home.

Experimental Architecture

Because the concept of shipping container homes *is* still relatively new, designers are still testing the limits of this type of architecture. There are many outlandish and truly avant-garde styles out there, and for adventurous potential homeowners, this may be the perfect option.

For a truly one-of-a-kind, boldly experimental look, present the challenge to a skilled architect or engineer. Should they be up to the task, this collaboration can result into a completely striking home design that has never been seen. A house like this will be an automatic conversation piece for whoever enters it.

Parting Words

Congratulations for reaching the end of this book!

Hopefully, this has been a sufficient introduction to the concept of shipping container homes, as well as a good preliminary source of knowledge in planning, designing, and building them. With any luck, this has inspired you to build your own shipping container home!

The next step is to seek out more resources and experienced building professionals to answer any lingering concerns or questions. You'll be ready to start your own construction project in no time.

Best of luck with your building!

Made in the USA
San Bernardino, CA
10 November 2016